Summary and Analysis of

THE LEAN STARTUP

Based on the Book by Eric Ries

WORTH BOOKS
SMART SUMMARIES

This Worth Books book is based on the 2011 hardcover edition of *The Lean Startup* by Eric Ries published by Crown Business.

Summary and analysis copyright © 2017 by Open Road Integrated Media, Inc.

ISBN: 978-1-5040-4671-8

Worth Books
180 Maiden Lane
Suite 8A
New York, NY 10038
www.worthbooks.com

WORTH BOOKS
SMART SUMMARIES

Worth Books is a division of Open Road Integrated Media, Inc.

Contents

Context

Lean manufacturing, a concept pioneered by Toyota and based on the process-flow ideology of Henry Ford, is a system in which each segment of a process adds value to the whole, and none of the parts cause waste. In other words, lean manufacturing seeks to eliminate waste while increasing value to the consumer.

The principles of lean manufacturing have been appropriated for use in various industries. Author Eric Ries, a veteran of numerous tech launches, applies the "lean" concept to startups. Ironically, it was through his experience of business failure that he developed the methodology put forth in his bestselling book, *The Lean Startup: How Today's Entrepreneurs Use*

Continuous Innovation to Create Radically Successful Businesses.

Ries began a blog about his experiences called *Startup Lessons Learned* and spoke to conferences and companies interested in employing his methods. The Lean Startup concept eventually sparked a movement that led to the development of the book. Published in 2011, *The Lean Startup* was an enormous success, and the notions Ries put forth have been widely discussed and adopted in the years since. Lean Startup Company, which Ries cofounded, has held a yearly "Lean Startup Week" since 2010 to assist entrepreneurs with implementing lean thinking into their businesses.

Overview

The Lean Startup is a book about efficiency. Entrepreneurs are not in a race with other companies or even themselves. According to Eric Ries, their biggest rival is time. Since there's no way to create more time, the question becomes how to save as much of it as possible. Ries urges startups to employ a more scientific approach, continually testing and tweaking their process as they go. He encourages entrepreneurs to give up on ideas that can't be supported by data. By abandoning a project that's doomed, you don't waste time going down a path that you should already know is a dead end.

Ries discusses his own startup experiences in Silicon Valley, both the failures and the successes. These experiences were the foundation of what became his Lean Startup method. He details the lean manufacturing movement pioneered by Toyota, and uses examples from many well-known digital brands such as Facebook, Dropbox, and PayPal. In addition, he looks at the seemingly minor evolutions of products that illuminate the larger ideas of lean thinking.

Summary

Introduction

Ries describes the Lean Startup method and how he developed it. There are five basic ideas behind this approach:

1. Anyone, anywhere, can be an entrepreneur. Contrary to the popular definition, Ries defines a startup as any group attempting to make a new product or service in an unpredictable environment. Thus, anyone running such an enterprise is an entrepreneur.

2. The management of the startup is as important as the product itself. The concepts of

"entrepreneurship" and "management" cannot be separated.

3. Since startups are inherently untested, being new products or ideas, they require a continual state of learning in order to be successful. Ries uses the term "validated learning" to describe this cycle of testing.

4. There is a standard process that startups should follow: "Build-Measure-Learn." Ries believes companies should first make a product, see how consumers react to it, and then take action in response. This cycle continues throughout the building of the business.

5. No matter how exciting and fresh its product is, a startup needs to do the dull work of quantifying progress.

Part One: VISION

1. Start

There are more entrepreneurial opportunities today than at any other time in human history. But because we use antiquated management techniques, startups are not getting the most out of our human resources and, worse, they are "achieving failure"—a phrase Ries uses to describe the perfect execution of a plan to build something that it turns out nobody wants or needs. Rather than make something and wait to see if it attracts customers, businesses should use scientific methods to determine what customers want before they spend a lot of time and money creating a perfect product.

2. Define

Any type of entrepreneur in almost any industry can use the Lean Startup philosophy to increase the likelihood of launching a successful startup. What makes a startup different from other businesses isn't that the business is related to technology, necessarily. It's that the new service or product is framed by extreme uncertainty—that is, there is no known business model and no known market for the product. Ries uses the example of Intuit's SnapTax to illustrate that a startup can even exist within an established business. Customers who were using Intuit's TurboTax began asking if there was a way to complete their taxes entirely on their phones. Seizing this opportunity, Intuit was able to develop such a product while still maintaining its core business with TurboTax.

3. Learn

A startup must measure progress, but knowing the right way to measure progress is critical. If a business is failing, entrepreneurs will often spin it as a learning experience. While doubtlessly true, that doesn't change the fact that the exercise is a waste of time and money. It's not surprising, therefore, that "learning" has something of a bad reputation in business. In spite of this, it is a vital piece of the startup process.

Ries reconceives "learning" to make the process an actual, quantifiable part of product development. He calls this "validated learning," meaning that each experiment leads to an improvement in the process or an improvement to the product (and therefore validates the time and money spent on learning). It helps a startup understand how close its vision is to what customers want—which may be very different from what the creators originally imagined. According to Ries, validated learning requires a scientific approach to measure results and test hypotheses.

4. Experiment

Learning is impossible if there isn't a way to fail without catastrophic consequences. To determine which parts of a startup's strategy are good and which are bad, it is more efficient to run a series of experiments than to waste resources on surveys and market research. Ries cites examples of this approach from Zappos and Kodak, as well as within government and volunteer programs. He posits that data from small-batch experiments that target early adopters is the best way to learn about which aspects of a product or process work, and which do not. People using an actual product are able to offer more valuable feedback than people being asked questions about a hypothetical product. Additionally, the product itself has already been built and tested in this process, so it's ready for tweaking.

Part Two: STEER

This section examines the best way to move through the Build-Measure-Learn feedback loop as quickly as possible.

Essentially, a startup begins with an idea for a product, then builds that product. Once constructed, the product undergoes the testing discussed in previous chapters, which provides data that allows the startup to learn. The learning, as we've seen, leads to ideas about how to improve or change the product. At this point, the entire loop begins again. For efficiency's sake, the startup must cycle through this loop as fast as it can.

5. Leap

The author uses the early days of Facebook to illustrate two invaluable ideas behind any successful startup:

the value hypothesis and the growth hypothesis. To attract investors, a startup must be able to offer not only value (a product that customers want), but also the prospect of continued growth (a product that will continue to add value going forward). If a startup can offer an answer to these two hypotheses, that startup can then take a "leap of faith" to begin work.

As we've seen in previous chapters, testing is vital to success. Even the basic leap-of-faith assumptions must be tested. The Japanese phrase *genchi gembutsu* speaks to how this must be done. It means "go and see for yourself." Ries describes how this method is utilized by Toyota to gain firsthand knowledge of consumer needs. It is not enough to do traditional market research; the entrepreneur must literally talk to customers in order to develop solutions for the problem the startup aims to solve.

6. Test

This chapter details the concept of the "minimum viable product" (MVP), which is the fastest way for entrepreneurs to engage in the Build-Measure-Learn loop. The MVP is not a prototype in the traditional sense, because it is built not to approximate the final product, but rather to answer questions about technical aspects, design, and business hypotheses.

An MVP doesn't need to be perfect; its role is to

test the entrepreneur's assumptions about a product based on its interaction with early adopters. MVPs often deliver bad news, which is just as important as good news, and which is the reason a cheaper, more basic version of the product was built first. Worried about the competition stealing the idea? Ries assures the reader that, for the most part, the competition either won't care or won't be able to do anything about it.

7. Measure

Accounting is important to all business ventures. But the typical methods of accounting cannot be applied to startups because of the degree of uncertainty involved in the process. Therefore, Ries suggests that startups use what he calls "innovation accounting." The first step in this accounting process is to build the MVP and test it, as seen in chapter six. With the data gained by testing the MVP, the startup can establish an accurate picture of where it stands. Once this baseline exists, the next step is to "tune the engine," as Ries puts it. That means looking at where the product is and at where it ultimately needs to be, and then making incremental changes to get it there. Along the way, of course, the process of validated learning continues. Eventually this data will make clear whether the startup is moving toward its ideal or away from it. At that point, a decision can be made: keep going, or fundamentally change the product or process?

Measuring progress this way is critical for startups. Whether a startup will succeed or fail is exceedingly difficult to predict, and this is made more difficult because so many of them rely on vanity metrics—numbers created specifically to make it look as if the company is doing well. These metrics are often given to investors or the media, but the danger is when the startup itself believes in the vanity metrics.

Using IMVU and Grockit as examples, Ries discusses many different methods of gathering actionable metrics—that is, numbers that directly show the results of specific actions. These metrics, not vanity metrics, must be used to evaluate the product and make decisions. Some of the methods described are split-testing, cohort analysis, and *kanban*, which is a Japanese term for constraining capacity.

8. Pivot (or Persevere)

Once the right information has been gathered through methods such as the MVP, the Build-Measure-Learn loop, and innovation accounting, the fit between the product and the market is known. This allows a startup to intelligently change direction rather than, say, mistakenly fire its management team. It might mean pivoting toward a product nobody envisioned, but this is preferable to the course too many entrepreneurs take: refusing to admit their original course was flawed, which leads to the failure of the entire company.

When pivoting, the entrepreneur does not blindly change to a new product or process. Rather, they use the information gained through the all the previous testing to lead them in a new direction that offers sustainable growth.

Part Three: ACCELERATE

Once a startup has decided to persevere—to move forward with its product—it is time to accelerate. This does not mean that the learning feedback loop ends, but rather that the information gained is used to create a company that utilizes lean thinking as its backbone as it moves into the future.

9. Batch

Startups should think big about products but think small about batches. Most people would think the fastest way to manufacture something is to create an assembly line that does each task separately. But in fact, it has been proven more efficient to use a "single-piece flow," which means that one product is made in its entirety before the next is begun.

The value of the single-piece flow is that errors aren't proliferated throughout a large batch. If step three on your assembly line requires a screw to be dropped into a hole, but the hole has been drilled in the wrong place in step one, the error will not be discovered until the batch reaches step three. All of the products already on the line will have to be scrapped, since their holes are in the wrong place. By contrast, if one product in its entirety is completed before moving on to the next one, that error will be discovered on the first round. Waste is reduced, and the problem will be addressed more quickly.

For startups, utilizing small batches allows problems to be spotted and fixed rapidly. The small batch concept is also built into the MVP. Tech companies can borrow from Toyota's *andon* cord, which allows any member of the team to shut down production when a problem is detected. Picture that assembly line: you don't want it to keep chugging along, drilling holes in the wrong place. You want to stop the line immediately until the problem is addressed. When this thinking is applied to the Build-Measure-Learn loop, it saves time and money while improving systemic quality.

10. Grow

Growth alone isn't enough. Startups must seek sustainable growth, which means continually finding new markets and new customers. The best way to do this is to use existing customers, who contribute to growth by talking about the product, using the product so that others can see it, buying the product for repeat use, and, at the most basic level, paying for the product. The money made on past purchases is what pays for the advertising that creates new customers.

Ries discusses three engines of growth: viral, sticky, and paid. While it is possible for a company to run more than one engine at a time, he feels that the most prosperous startups use only one. The process of *genchi gembutsu* is a good way for a startup to decide which growth engine is most appropriate for them. Making small adjustments after each Build-Measure-Learn loop is the way to achieve a better fit between the product and the market.

11. Adapt

There are many more ways for startups to fail than to succeed. The entire organization must be adaptive to new challenges—and it must stay adaptive. Ries says that one important way to do this is for managers to incentivize group success over individual success. Doing the reverse may result in a situation where office politics stifles innovation. The long-term prospects of a company are grim unless employees feel they'll sink or swim together.

It is also important to make sure employees are trained properly so that they can be successful at adapting. How to tell if the training is effective? Ries suggests using a method called the Five Whys. Borrowed from Toyota, the philosophy of the Five Whys says that when there is a problem, the root will be discovered when you ask "why?" five times. Ries uses the example of a problem with the new version of a product that's just been released: *"1. A new release disabled a feature for customers. Why? Because a particular server failed. 2. Why did the server fail? Because an obscure subsystem was used in the wrong way. 3. Why was it used in the wrong way? The engineer who used it didn't know how to use it properly. 4. Why didn't he know? Because he was never trained. 5. Why wasn't he trained? Because his manager doesn't believe in training new engineers because he and his team are 'too busy.'"* As we see in this example, the process of asking questions reveals a simple, human problem, even if the trouble initially seems to be technical.

But use caution: if this technique isn't employed properly, people may use it to shift the blame (five times). Done correctly, the Five Whys can reveal unwelcome issues: a problem with the management or process, for example. It is crucial that these problems are seen and corrected. Ries stresses the importance of solving a problem using a proportionate amount of resources—a small outlay of resources for a small problem, a large outlay for a large problem.

12. Innovate

Companies can still act like startups as they grow, and they should. Creativity and innovation are a vital part of any organization, and retaining lean thinking can help with this even after the flagship product no longer carries with it the uncertainty required to be considered a startup.

One way to do this is to allow small teams to operate independently within a larger organization. But the parent organization must not feel threatened by the startup. Consider developing what Ries calls an "innovation sandbox," a small area of the main product (or process) that innovative teams are encouraged to openly experiment on. As long as the experiment is contained to that one area, it cannot harm the company's main product, and it may lead to the development of something new and beneficial to the company as a whole.

13. Epilogue: Waste Not

There is a great deal of waste in modern business. While our ability to manufacture virtually anything is greater than ever before in history, the problem remains that it is wasteful to make things that are not needed. Ries wants us to stop asking whether or not a product can be built and start asking whether or not it *should* be built. The lean startup seeks to reduce the waste created by expending resources on the wrong ideas—those that do not fill a demand or solve a problem. It is not a matter of making workers more productive or efficient, because they already are both of those things. Rather, it is a matter of using their efficiency to create products that people actually want.

The focus should not be on how hard a business works—it should be on working more intelligently. This means valuing facts over intuition, science over pseudoscience. Ries warns against allowing lean thinking to become a system in and of itself: testing and learning, he stresses, cannot continue in a rigid system.

Cast of Characters

Caroline Barlerin: Former director in the global social innovation division at Hewlett-Packard, where Ries said she tried to inspire the people she worked with to make the world a better place. Barlerin used Lean Startup principles in her efforts to expand volunteerism among Hewlett-Packard employees.

David Binetti: Entrepreneur and former CEO of Votizen who used innovation accounting to improve the speed with which his startup pivoted in order to become a successful business.

Steve Blank: Serial tech entrepreneur who wrote *The Four Steps to the Epiphany* and created the Customer Development methodology, which contributed to Ries's development of *The Lean Startup*. Blank also required Ries to audit his class at UC Berkeley's Haas School of Business before investing in one of Ries's ventures. That class helped inspire the Lean Startup movement.

Scott Cook: Cofounder of Intuit, which develops software for taxes and finances. Cook invited Ries to speak to all Intuit employees about the Lean Startup methodology, demonstrating that even established companies like Intuit could also benefit from lean thinking. Cook also proved that large businesses can stay agile when Intuit developed SnapTax, a startup within a bigger company.

Damon Horowitz and Max Ventilla: Cofounders of Aardvark. They used a series of MVPs and took six months to test them before deciding exactly what to build. Taking their time to experiment paid off when Google acquired the company.

Drew Houston: Founder of Dropbox who used a video MVP to help launch the billion-dollar company.

Jeffrey Liker: Professor of Industrial and Operations Engineering at the University of Michigan, and an expert on Toyota's Production System. He's also written several books about Japanese management techniques, including *The Toyota Way*.

Taiichi Ohno: Father of the Toyota Production System, whose book about it began what became known as "lean manufacturing." Ohno also developed the Five Whys.

Manuel Rosso: Founder of Food on the Table, a culinary startup. He developed a concierge MVP, which is a personalized service that helps entrepreneurs test the leap-of-faith assumptions in their company's growth model.

Shigeo Shingo: Toyota Production System manufacturing expert who worked with Taiichi Ohno. Shingo created the Single-Minute Exchange of Die (SMED), which fostered smaller batch sizes in early Toyota factories, and redesigned many other machines to reduce changeover times from hours to less than ten minutes.

Direct Quotes and Analysis

"The goal of a startup is to figure out the right thing to build—the thing customers want and will pay for—as quickly as possible. In other words, the Lean Startup is a new way of looking at the development of innovative new products that emphasizes fast iteration and customer insight, a huge vision, and great ambition, all at the same time."

Too many startups waste time by developing products nobody wants. Even if the project is done perfectly—on time and on budget, meeting every production goal—it will all be for nothing if the finished product doesn't sell. The Lean Startup methodology seeks to solve this problem by changing the way entrepreneurs think about development. By involving consumers in the process earlier through the use of MVPs and validated learning, a lean startup rapidly figures out if there is a demand for its product.

"[A startup is] a human institution designed to create new products or services under conditions of extreme uncertainty."

What differentiates a startup from other types of new businesses is the fact that a startup faces entirely new problems and an entirely new market—indeed, it is frequently unclear if a market for the product exists at all. Companies in established industries have a preexisting set of expectations and market data. A startup must learn—and learn quickly—whether its product or service is marketable, and it can do this using the Lean Startup method.

"We must learn what customers really want, not what they say they want or what we think they should want."

Traditional market research is not useful for startups because potential customers lack any experience with the product. Consumer feedback is far more valuable when it concerns a real product rather than a hypothetical product. This is why building an MVP and engaging in validated learning is so important.

"[The] Build-Measure-Learn feedback loop is at the core of the Lean Startup model."

In order to create a product that customers want, quickly and efficiently, a lean startup must move through this loop, over and over again, improving the product and the process each time. The loop begins with an idea, and an MVP must be built very quickly to begin testing that idea. Once there is an MVP, early adopters can provide true, measurable data that can be used to come up with ideas to improve the product, and the loop begins again.

"The only way to win is to learn faster than anyone else."

If a startup is a success, it will eventually face competition no matter how big its head start is. Therefore, the way to stay ahead of competitors is to move more quickly through the feedback loop so as to continuously improve the product.

"The big question of our time is not Can it be built? but Should it be built? This places us in an unusual historical moment: our future prosperity depends on the quality of our collective imaginations."

Over the past century, there was a focus on developing theories of management and efficiency, generally in service of creating goods to meet basic human needs. Ries states that now we have entered a new phase, one in which is there is no limit on what we can build—the only limit is our imagination. That's why it's important to figure out whether a product is needed or not. To spend time creating a good or service that no one needs is a tremendous waste of resources.

"Beyond simple research, I believe our goal should be to change the entire ecosystem of entrepreneurship."

Ries would like to see a substantial change in the way startups function in the business world. Instead of building products simply to sell them to large, established companies, he wants startups to structure themselves so as to focus on long-term thinking. In this way, the Lean Startup philosophy of creativity and innovation can be maintained.

Trivia

1. Despite the continuous loss of manufacturing jobs in the United States, total manufacturing output has doubled in three decades.

2. Eric Ries's popular blog *Startup Lessons Learned* was the forerunner to *The Lean Startup*.

3. Toyota, which developed many of the systems advocated by Ries in this book, became the world's largest automaker in 2008 when it surpassed General Motors. GM had been number one since the early 1930s.

4. Taiichi Ohno developed the Five Whys for the Toyota Production System.

5. Nine out of ten startups fail.

6. In 2004, Steve Blank insisted that Eric Ries and Will Harvey take his class at UC Berkeley before he would agree to invest in IMVU.

What's That Word?

Andon **cord:** A system that allows any worker to stop production and ask for help as soon as a problem is found.

Build-Measure-Learn loop: The fastest way to test a product to ensure that it matches with its intended market.

Cohort analysis: This type of analysis evaluates groups of customers separately from cumulative totals. It is useful because it isolates the behaviors that are most important to test a particular aspect of the product or the process.

The Five Whys: A technique developed by Toyota's Taiichi Ohno to solve problems systematically. It ensures that the right problems are being addressed in order to prevent future issues of the same kind. By asking "why" five times, and following the answers, you can almost always get to the real root of a problem.

Genchi gembutsu: A Japanese phrase that means "go and see for yourself." Firsthand knowledge informs a startup's strategy by deepening the understanding of the problem that the product aims to solve.

Growth hypothesis: A startup's plan for how new customers will discover a product or service.

Innovation accounting: A way for startups to measure progress that focuses on milestone-based learning rather than more traditional methods.

Kanban: A principle borrowed from Toyota's lean manufacturing, it restrains capacity for the purpose of validated learning.

Minimum Viable Product (MVP): The simplest version of a product that allows the most information to be gathered with the least amount of effort.

Pivot: A change of course that examines a new hypothesis about a strategy, product, or engine of growth.

Split testing: A controlled, randomized experiment that determines which of two versions of a product— usually, a webpage—yields the better results. (Also known as A/B testing.)

Startup: A newly established business that is able to scale quickly and faces risks established businesses do not.

Validated learning: Learning through a process of scientifically testing each element of a startup's vision.

Value hypothesis: A startup's perceived value of a product or service for customers.

Critical Response

- An Amazon Best Business Book of 2011
- A *New York Times* bestseller

"Every so often a business book comes along that changes how we think about innovation and entrepreneurship. . . . Eric Ries's *The Lean Startup* has the chops to join this exalted company."

—*Financial Times*

"After reading half a chapter of the book, the message hit me in the face like a ton of bricks. . . . It took me a million dollars to learn the basic ideas of the book. After one quick reading, I became a preacher of the book."

—Jason Saltzman,
CEO of Alley

"The Lean methodology is the closest thing to a scientific approach to startup creation that we have."
—*Tech Crunch*

"There's a whole industry devoted to promulgating the myth that all an entrepreneur needs is perseverance, creative genius, and hard work. Ries learned the hard way this isn't true."   —*Fast Company*

"The concepts apply both to designing products and to developing a market, and emphasize an early and constant focus on customers." —*The New York Times*

"The key lesson of this book is that startups happen in the present—that messy place between the past and the future where nothing happens according to PowerPoint. Ries's 'read and react' approach to this sport, his relentless focus on validated learning, the never-ending anxiety of hovering between 'persevere' and 'pivot,' all bear witness to his appreciation for the dynamics of entrepreneurship."   —Geoffrey Moore, author of *Crossing the Chasm*

About Eric Ries

Eric Ries left Yale to chase his first startup dream. It failed. He finished school and went right back to Silicon Valley, where he is now a bestselling author and entrepreneur.

While an undergraduate at Yale, Ries started a social network for students that sounded an awful lot like another dorm-room tech company at a rival Ivy League school. Ries has said that the early days of Catalyst Recruiting played out much like the story of Facebook. His story, of course, did not end the same way.

His next venture, There.com, also failed. But with a There.com cofounder, Will Harvey, Ries tried his hand at another social network, IMVU. It still exists today, and the lessons he took from his time developing that platform inform his work as an author, speaker, and advisor.

For Your Information

Online

"Can You Teach Entrepreneurship?" Mashable.com

"Eric Ries, the Face of the Lean Startup Movement, on How a Once-Insane Idea Went Mainstream." Xconomy.com

"Interview: Eric Ries, Author Of *The Lean Startup*." Wired.com

"Lean Innovation: Design Thinking Meets Lean Startup for the Enterprise." Forbes.com

TheLeanStartup.com

"The Rise of the Fleet-Footed Start-Up." NYTimes.com

StartupLessonsLearned.com

"Why I Back Eric Ries Over Peter Thiel." Entrepreneur.com

Books

The Four Steps to the Epiphany by Steve Blank

Business Adventures by John Brooks

Live Free or DIY by Justin E. Crawford

The Innovator's Dilemma: When New Technologies Cause Great Firms to Fail by Clayton M. Christensen

The Toyota Way: 14 Management Principles from the World's Greatest Manufacturer by Jeffrey K. Liker

Toyota Production System: Beyond Large-Scale Production by Taiichi Ohno

Zero to One: Notes on Startups, or How to Build the Future by Peter Thiel and Blake Masters

WORTH BOOKS
SMART SUMMARIES

So much to read, so little time?

Explore summaries of bestselling fiction and essential nonfiction books on a variety of subjects, including business, history, science, lifestyle, and much more.

Visit the store at
www.ebookstore.worthbooks.com

MORE SMART SUMMARIES
FROM WORTH BOOKS

BUSINESS

WORTH BOOKS
SMART SUMMARIES

OPEN ROAD
INTEGRATED MEDIA

CPSIA information can be obtained
at www.ICGtesting.com
Printed in the USA
LVHW112228271021
701762LV00005B/138

9 781504 046718